What Does Love See?

By Jan Kovac

What Does Love See?

www.whatdoeslovesee.com

Published by Free To Be One Publishing

Acknowledgements

Gratitude is a quality that is expressed out of love and real appreciation. It is with that kind of gratitude that I thank the wonderful people in my life.

Everyone has been a teacher from my parents and siblings to my school teachers, friends and especially family. When I began to awaken to some truth in my life I was given counselors like Dr. R. Merkle and Ann and Jan Linthorst. Marjorie Dagnall has been a Christian Science practitioner always available as a guide, as well.

To my friend Barbara Quilliam who has supported my writings with encouragement and her typing skills – much love. Molly Hardy is a fellow writer whose expertise has said, "Keep going." Laura Sonderegger, who generously shared her knowledge and skills in encouraging, formatting and publishing. And, Becky Stilling was the gift given on the way to engaging and completing, *What Does Love See?* She has been editor and companion these last two years always reminding me that this is written from a higher awareness we both refer to as God.

Thank you all for being in my life!
Peace, Assurance, Gratitude, and Love
~ Jan Kovac

Foreword

What does Love see?
What kind of a question is that?

For Jan Kovac, that question emerged in her consciousness as the "search engine" of her life-long quest to find a way to see beyond her personal identity and its story.

Clearly, it came from Love, and as she explores her decades of struggle and revelation, it brings its fruits of Love when it is bravely attended to - no matter what the seeming scenarios of the story.

Jan shares her story, and the glad fruits of devotion to that question, in this honest and generous book. It is not a book to be read through and put on the shelf! Each section has been deeply researched by Jan in her own experience. And each section offers guidance for those who want to do their own exploration in quest of the answer to that shining question.

In describing that exploration, spiritual teacher Rupert Spira says, of the Love that is our own true Being, "Just turn toward Me, acknowledge Me, and I will take you into Myself."

This book gives the reader guidance in that sacred search.

- Ann Linthorst

Contents

Inspiration for Book Cover

"Are you a pilgrim drawn to the Light of understanding or a prisoner of life's experiences?"

Mont-St-Michel in France is a vision that takes your breath away. It was May 2015 when I was on a personal tour that I first saw the Gothic dwelling. The 13th century Abbey is surrounded by the sea with a tremendous tidal surge. It was even given the name, "Mount in Peril from the Sea" because so many pilgrims trying to reach that destination had vanished in the quicksand.

The magnificent view as we approached revealed a magical castle seemingly floating above the sea. In my imagination, it became a place of safety as a monastery and at the same time a secluded prison - clearly a choice in my perspective.

The tour inside the edifice led us through a Refectory where my eyes focused on a single window of bright sunlight surrounded by four feet thick granite walls. That light seemed to express warmth, comfort and love. It became a metaphor where the sunlight represented light overcoming darkness in our lives.

As I stood silently taking in the beauty of the light filling the room, I asked myself, “are you a pilgrim drawn to the Light of understanding or a prisoner of life’s experiences?” The invitation to see is always available throughout our lives.

Light and Dark

Standing on the cliff
Looking out to the sea,
I am overwhelmed by
The brightness of the setting sun.

Hot white and orange with
A golden yellow intensity
It pierces through
Approaching darkness

The Light so bright it
Travels as an arrow
Straight to
My open heart.

And all the while
Darkness waits
As light slowly disappears
With sundown.

But the piercing light
Shines even when
Darkness tries to
Take one under its spell.

Perhaps it's a metaphor
For Spiritual awakening.
We have the dark so we
Can see the light,

But it never overtakes us!
- *Jan Kovac*

An Invitation

*"**What Does Love See**?" is an invitation to look with new eyes, a new perspective. Ask yourself to go beyond your thinking mind into a realm of conscious awareness.*

If you are seeking joy and happiness outside yourself, look again! They are here and now within but you may have to take a journey of self-inquiry to finally see and feel the reality.

This book invites you to be present and notice your very own life unfolding perfectly for you!

Love, Jan

Prologue

Each of us has a story to tell – it is the story of our life. Each of us, from birth, has been saving into the personal computer of our mind what we perceive to be the truth about our life story. We are given and receive data from parents, teachers, siblings, friends, experiences and the environment. Whether we tell tales of love and happiness with laughter in our voices, or whether we sob out our tales of sorrow or horror or despair, we are telling the "real truth" about our lives as we see it. Our belief and faith in the "reality" of our lives, no matter how barren or tragic, seems set in concrete.

We often fight with great energy against the idea that there is another deeper reality, another truth, another light. We find it difficult to accept the fact that much of what we believe is an illusion, and we often are afraid to give up these illusions. It seems that we are afraid to risk allowing light to enter our lives, even if it will bring new life with it.

Many of us, however, come to a point in our lives when we know that we must search for a glimmer of light, a new path, a method of developing awareness and openness. We wish to become able to separate truth from illusion so that we can make choices. Finally, we find that a path does begin to unfold. Somehow, an unseen guide begins to light our way for us.

Often we go in groups of like-minded searchers – religious groups, for example, or support groups of various kinds. We may kick and scream and protest as we pursue our journey, as some of our most cherished "beliefs" are challenged, no matter how self-destructive they may be. But once we have made the choice that we wish to search for truth, spiritual truth, we will continue.

God is the ultimate place of rest and peace – light and truth. As St Augustine said, "Our heart is restless until it rests in thee".

The search for wholeness of body, mind and spirit is the quest of a lifetime. We all have free will, the will to choose. Once that choice is made, like-minded people seem to appear. A pathway opens to us and the journey of the soul consciously begins.

Introduction

This is my story,
but now I need to tell a different story!
What does Love see?

THE STORY

How many people say, "I want to write a book"? Everyone has a story to tell, some famous and some infamous. And then there is the ordinary man or woman who feels that sharing their life experience might just be something that encourages another ordinary person.

That's me, a wife, mother, nurse by profession, and a spiritual seeker for most of my life. I write poems and articles and keep journals for my growth. So a few years ago I compiled 35 years' worth of insights into a legacy book for my children and grandchildren.

Now, something more wants to be expressed. The public has experienced many spiritual teachers like Eckhart Tolle, Byron Katie, Wayne Dyer, and Deepak Chopra, assisting people to feel more comfortable with ideas that are broader than just religious ones.

We look for deeper meanings and are looking to live a more conscious life. Well, some of us are and the planet needs a higher awareness to be shown both within and without.

This book is expressing an idea that encourages the reader to use their very own life as the beginning and end of their search for deeper meaning.

You can learn from the situations that arise and you don't have to go follow someone else's life. Even in reading the stories of the life of Jesus I understood that he wasn't asking us to be blind followers of him but to seek the truth by discovering our oneness with Big Life.

All that said in one short paragraph sounds so easy, but it is just a pointer, a suggestion. You have to want to live a more peaceful, harmonious life and then have the courage to ask from your deepest yearning for help.

There are many paths, many religions and many teachers, but two things seem to be the consistent pointers for discovery. Pain pushes you and desiring to know the truth pulls you to open your heart. Then, with an honest and open heart, you follow.

I've had a counselor and spiritual guide for forty years, so I believe we all need help in the form of guidance. What I've learned is that we have to listen to the inner voice. Listening is the hard part. Once we realize there is more to life than that we're born to human parents, live in a human body and struggle and finally die, we become open to the bigger questions...

Sometimes we experience this awakening in midlife or when we've been through a life crisis. I started looking at these questions in my late twenties.

As a child, I had been religious and even "took myself" to church. They had grape juice and cookies and told me Jesus loved me. I was sold!

My teenage years came with zealous ideas and self-righteousness. My parents found me obnoxious I'm sure. But truth does not leave you where it finds you and the road to spiritual maturity had its way. You just have to grow up!

My profession was a Registered Nurse. When I was 18 years old, I found my training at a Catholic nursing school. I became interested in the nun's dedication to God and Mass. Mass was foreign to me but the mystery of it all was captivating.

In the middle of my training program, I met a very handsome sailor from the North and he was a Catholic. Now the story unfolds and finds this Southern girl in love and leaving her religion to explore another. Being twenty-one years old and in love took its natural course. I studied Catholicism and eventually joined the church and we married soon after.

At the time I was very religious and interested in God but at a distance. I attended church. I did what I was told and life seemed smooth enough, but I didn't let the vulnerability I felt interrupt my life. I kept all that questioning at a distance.

Immediately, the adventure of being newly married and having my first job in a hospital began in earnest. We had planned for Karl to attend The University of Texas with me as the primary breadwinner but life has its way it seems and I became pregnant. So, I would have another new task – mother.

Over the years we were blessed in many ways. He graduated and obtained an excellent job in New York. We moved our little family to many new locations as Karl's career advanced. This period of our lives felt extremely challenging but also brought material rewards. We had all the goodies in life but I still felt unrest and longing.

In my early 30s, I was at a cocktail party in my neighbor's back yard having a run-of-the-mill conversation with an acquaintance. She had made a statement and I responded that God would zap me if I did that. "Do you believe that?" she asked. "Yes, I do," I said after a long pause.

I had a fearsome God and he would punish me as He chose. I think that's the first crack in the eggshell of awakening.

I had always gone to church and was sure there was a God but here I saw what kind of God I believed in and worshipped. It was a childhood God up in the heavens somewhere that was punishing and unloving. Something happened to me with this kind of awareness. Deep inside there was unrest brought up to be felt.

After the birth of my third child, I felt another nudge. Who was God and who was I? Where did I fit in the scheme of big life? I had everything I thought you were supposed to acquire. I was in a beautiful place in life with the nursing profession I had worked so hard for, a handsome successful husband, and three healthy, beautiful children. We had a big home with a pool in sunny California, new friends; some money saved up and I even got my figure back after childbirth.

How could I be unhappy? But I was and it wouldn't go away. When you think you are the nurse, wife and mother kind of caregiver you notice and worry about others and their pain and suffering. This doesn't help your doubts and anxiety. These things combined made me susceptible to mild depression over the years.

What followed, and especially in the 1970s, with all the ideas of "improving yourself," I began to work to improve myself. Self-help books were everywhere and I even found a counselor I could trust. The counselor came after the psychiatrist that my husband felt was very unnecessary (*…how would that look to others and we didn't have the money to pay for one…*).

My sense of helplessness was too great to listen to him then (which I always did before) and I found someone else to listen to me without prescribing drugs.

In three months I had another "egg crack moment." I realized I had been seeing myself as a victim (a key step I later learned). In my subconscious thought, everyone from my parents, siblings, husband and the world **had done something to me**!

This was earth-shattering for this little, nice girl who had grown up through the 50s. Do you mean, I was responsible for where I was and how things looked? Maybe I didn't accept that totally, but I was willing to look now.

Once you are aware that life is much bigger than the beliefs you've lived with, you have to live a more alert life.

You still have the same place in the queue. I think the boredom with the repetition of everyday life begins to scream at you. You get up, brush your teeth and maybe your hair before you get the kids up and prepare breakfast for them and your traditional husband. He would work and make the money and I could do everything else.

Not many men shared household chores and helped with childcare during the 1960s, 70s and on into the 80s. We had a good marriage but he started his own business (his dream) and worked very long hours.

We did not have family nearby so support had to be found through friends and church. I think we moved nine times over our 42 years of marriage and each time it was up to me to create a new community for our family.

Grace carries you even if you don't recognize it.

When we settled into Orange County the right people, books and counselors soon appeared. Tustin, California was a sleepy community with good schools and we decided to make this town our home where we would raise our three precious children.

Now in my mid-thirties, I realized there was an angry woman hidden deep inside. My mother was angry and her mother probably was. My grandmother had thirteen children and even though I was born after she died, I'm pretty sure she worked hard and had little support and appreciation. Maybe she too was an angry woman!

One of my first new friends referred me to a counselor's group sessions where he had a series on constructive emotions. I was anxious to find out if something good could be discovered from anger.

At that time I was introduced to a teacher who wrote a book called "Beyond the Dream". As I studied, went to group meetings and read that book I realized where I struggled in life was not unusual and that struggling was actually good. What a relief!

In 1980 I was faced with the results of my mother's COPD which brought her to an early death. I felt frustrated that the doctors had not helped her more and had not listened to her at all. My assumption was they did not listen, but maybe she did not share.

I was now willing to look beyond western medicine and religion for some new insight into healing and life in general. I went through a program called Health Facilitation where a forward-thinking husband and wife team (as doctor and nurse respectively) had created a three-year state-accredited program.

Many people from various healing disciplines attended and after three years graduated. We were the forerunners of the wellness centers, I think. Our function would be as health care and religious professionals and therapists to listen to and help clients who needed more direction other than a pill and a quick consult. We were health facilitators who were trained to be good listeners.

After graduation, there was a clinic opened by the group and I participated on staff but it did not take off as all had hoped. Following that, my attempts to offer services at a counseling service were received poorly, probably due to the new idea and my lack of deeper understanding. Over the last 25-30 years, I have provided groups with a spiritual focus related to physical health and healing. Having spent years studying the healing work of spiritual healers and being trained as a nurse and Health Facilitator, I saw the need for good listening in the medical system.

My children are grown, my husband passed away from a serious terminal illness and I'm a grandmother and even a great grandmother. Life looks virtually the same, I'm just older. But in reality, my whole existence is different from beginning to end.

What occurs to me now is that I had always used my own life to research Big Life. I just had not seen so clearly as I do now -- **Life** is living me.

So now I ask, "What does Love see, beyond my personal story and yours?"

So now I ask,
"What does Love see,
beyond my
personal story
and beyond yours?

Chapter I: Life Asks a New Question

Beginning to move from suffering to understanding

The human story lived and told can be of help to others who are looking more deeply for meaning in their lives. "What does **Love** see - not what do **I** see" becomes the bigger invitation.

For most of us, the searching begins when we are tapped on the shoulder by an event that threatens the status quo of our lives. We find ourselves in a predicament without any answers.

Sitting down defeated you begin to ask, "Is this all there is to life?" More questions surface:

- "Who am I and why am I here in this body at this time?"
- "Do I have a purpose in life?"
- "If all one does is exist just to survive, what's the point of living?"
- "Where is creativity?"

But, the presence of these feelings and questions is a good sign because something has been awakened inside you!

When you are born you are named and the indoctrination into personhood begins in full force. Like myself and everyone else on the planet, you have been taught to think of yourself as a person with a core belief that you are fundamentally alone, vulnerable and responsible for your own happiness - battling forces that could harm or destroy you.

This belief drives us to construct a personality or ego. Without knowing it we create a mask or shell that we put on to help us cope with our fears and make sure that we get what we need. Eventually, the mask starts to fail to do its job and this leads us to believe that we have failed. We might feel small, weak, guilty, confused and alone.

I was in this wilderness for a portion of my adult life. I often found this period in life emotionally painful and it drove me to question my long-held thoughts and beliefs. I began to sincerely seek peace and harmony – letting go of my impulse to insist I already knew how to live life.

The only way I knew to deal with the longing and sadness was to dig deep and question my thoughts. I decided that this should include working with a spiritually oriented guide and counselor. I had to face myself head-on and discover who I really was.

If you have a bigger question out of an inner awakening it helps to have a guide or therapist. Through grace, I was provided a spiritually based counselor and so my path was set in that direction.

Journaling became of utmost importance. All the fearful, negative, unloving thoughts running through my mind would often take me down the wrong road. But when the thoughts came up to me to be seen I wrote them down and they were exposed as lies. This process built new self-confidence and self-assurance.

I began to see that I am not my thoughts and I don't have to believe everything I think.

What followed was the beginning of experiencing peace and a beautiful sense of freedom! Awakening to real life, I began to see through my ego personality and experience a growing desire for Truth. This is where I became honest with myself which led to self-acceptance.

But there is more! Even after 40 years of counseling and spiritual searching for something greater to be seen, it took a simple and beautiful suggestion to change the paradigm of my life. I was invited to begin to ask, "What does **Love** see?"

It may sound strange but this was such a new angle on the question of my existence, I was dumbfounded! Instead of ruminating over how my personal sense (my ego) views a situation, this idea suggested that I could see life through a different set of eyes – the eyes of **Love**.

My true self realized that my life was not about me as a personality – not about a little me against the world, struggling for good (or perfection?) in my life. Instead, I was able to see that my life is an expression of **Love**. And, **Love** is constantly and eternally demonstrating intelligence, joy, beauty, harmony, peace and much more!

At this point, I began to feel I was a spiritual being having a human experience. I had to see that instead of studying man to know God, I needed to study God to know man as he truly is.

> *We know how much God loves us, and we have put our trust in his love.* ***God is love****, and all who live in love live in God, and God lives in them.* (1 John 4:16)

I tell you my story, dear reader, for you to have an idea about how to start telling yours. You have to stop and look at who you thought you were before you can start to see a new way of life. Life is living itself perfectly in a form you have called "me".

There is so much more when life lives itself.

Chapter I - *PAUSE PAGE*

The Pause Page is provided
for you to write your own reflections

Give some thought to:

Who am I?

What am I?

Where Am I?

What is my purpose in life?

(Psalm: 119:18); (Romans 12:2)

Chapter II: Who am I?

Am I living life too small?

Once you've recognized you have a story to tell of who you called "me", you have enough distance to SEE. Then you begin to ask, "*WHO AM* I really if I'm not my story?"

That may be our life's work – to stay awake to who we are - when the habit of personality tries to live our lives. So let's go deeper and examine the God you've carried inside most of your existence. What is he/she? And if seen, is it a mature God or, do you still have an immature vision of God (as in what or who you worship)?

When you are open to this question of how mature your understanding is, often other people come into your life with the same question. At this moment, a friend and I are sitting on my sofa discussing our childhood and how religion impacted us. We both grew up in small towns, she in California and I in Texas. We both believed that God was vengeful! But laughing at ourselves now we begin to see that we had covered up some old pain we buried from our past.

We had created a view of life based on our narrow-minded beliefs about God and the universe. Now, we are welcoming more mature ideas of a universe of love and a God of compassion.

So, maybe the first step in seeing life in a bigger context is the recognition of seeing a life too small. Your religion could be any belief that gives allegiance to an organized group of people with a rigid set of rules (e.g. religion, politics or family). You may find you based your entire life story on living under a fear-based belief about God or any other outside authority.

Are you presently living in
a world of your own making
where being loved and
accepted depends on how
perfect you are?

Your inner dialogue about evil, sin and God gives you a clue about who you think you are now. Have you created a god that is too small? Have you decided you are agnostic or atheist? Perhaps you do believe in a god (or gods) and count yourself as a theist. Regardless, is a certain belief running your life?

Atheism involves what a person does or does not believe. Agnosticism involves what a person does or does not know. These ideas should raise very big questions about how you hold your precious life. Do they provide the potential for greater understanding? Or, do these concepts just give you something to label yourself with so that you can stop struggling over your intimate existential questions?

Whether or not we feel a compelling need to search for truth, it's healthy for us to be curious, to solve life's riddles and question what we think we know. It's been discovered that this helps us to retain and improve our cognitive capabilities and to develop real wisdom and understanding.

When we don't do this, our world gets too small and we shortchange ourselves. Inevitably, there is one question we cannot avoid. Are we mortal? Do we really just suffer and struggle in life with a little happiness scattered throughout our short lives and then die – the end? Or, are we immortal? In my journey, I had so many questions.

There was a vibrancy
I wanted to embrace
so I continued to
look deeper within myself.

Many of us are wounded by what we feel religion taught and we shut down in pain with little understanding - saying, "No, no more to that god where acceptance, comfort or love cannot be found".

The god you took on is of your own making and it is too small in every way. So, with that thought, you threw the baby out with the bath water. You threw out the very thing that you had hoped to see and understand – LOVE.

There is emptiness and longing but you fill it with mundane things. You work too hard and dull your senses with food and drink. Or, you buy things that only make you happy for the moment. Or maybe you focus on your body and health and spend all of your extra time at the gym or the doctor.

These diversions may work for a long time but if you are blessed, something wakes you up. Most of us have to lose something we cherish and then suffer in our souls. We feel desolate.

For me, it was not sudden but a slow emerging dissatisfaction with the "stuff of life". I did everything I thought <u>they</u> said to do to be happy. What was wrong? I was still looking outside myself for approval and direction as a separate self (an ego).

I had good health, a career, a husband I loved, children I adored, a beautiful home and many friends. With all that, I still felt empty. I went to church faithfully and thought I was a good Christian. What was wrong? My god was way too small. I was an immature seeker of truth. I didn't seek – I thought I knew. I heard it said later that it's better to know you don't know than to be asleep to reality and think you do know.

This nagging dissatisfaction was necessary. It created an opening for truth. Finally with that awareness of dissatisfaction came a deep yearning to know the Truth about life and how I fit into the scheme of things.

What does Love see?
Not what does my
separate self (or ego) see?

Living with our everyday idea of "me" (a separate being) creates unending trouble and complications. Can we possibly have too narrow a view of life? I'd have to say "yes" as a witness to my own maturing and seeing all the immaturity and conflict in the world.

What possibility is there for change and growth if we start from a premise of separateness and only value our own story? Is there more? What does an immature god have to do with anything? It looks like the world has turned its back on honesty, integrity and God.

Everything looks like it's turned upside down as far as values in every arena from family to world values. The internet has connected us so we see in seconds "the other". How can we see the One? These are all sobering questions to have as we ask, "How mature is my concept of God. How mature am I?"

The scripture, "where your treasure is there will your heart be also" (Matthew 6:21), somehow began to reveal to me some insight and response to these questions. We seem to be born as separate little persons needing others to just survive.

Eventually, **our** patterns emerge: wanting to please, be accepted and approved of, we develop **our** masks and manage to develop **our** skills to control **our own** lives. We begin to treasure our personal life which we make into a personal god.

Is there more?
What does Love see?

Chapter II -*PAUSE PAGE*

Am I mature?

What does that mean to me?

Can I go deeper?

How do I view mortality…?

(1 Corinthians 13:1)

Chapter III: Looking Within

Self-Inquiry

Can you really use your own life in self-inquiry to grow deeper? Just who are you? Are you just a person/ego personality or are you a spiritual being with divine qualities - seeing that Life is living you?

With honesty and deep sincerity, you can look at your own story.

Stephen Karpman introduced the idea that the ego involved in relationship drama has three possible positions. He calls this a triangle of roles that you can take on and live as a victim, a persecutor or a rescuer. Some days you are all three but always in the box of life too small as a little personal self.

When you are in the drama, the neon signs of daily life flash, "NO EXIT"![1] But when you begin to see that you are playing a role, it begins to dawn on you that you have a choice.

---

[1] No Exit by Jean-Paul Sartre

The choice is Grace saying, "Take a step out of this straitjacket – risk that something more is living you." Along the way, we come to believe that we must work and strive to get what we need in life.

We are told that if there is a God out there, you had to be good enough and beg hard enough to get what you wanted in life. Now a glimmer of light and hope grows into the brightness of great expectancy of how life is really lived.

> *"The greatest and most important discovery in life – a discovery that anyone can make – is to discover that our essential nature does not share the limits or the destiny of the body and mind; and that peace, happiness and love are ever present within our own being, completely available at every moment of experience under all conditions." (*Rupert Spira)

In asking you to write your story, you are invited to begin to see your own themes and allow new modes of being to emerge. Are you always the victim when you tell your story? Does it change with who you are talking to at any given moment? Notice you may act and talk differently with family members than you do at work.

You begin to be a detective of sorts, but in a fun way without judgment. And if you begin to journal and note these things in a curious and playful way, many secrets are revealed.

As you begin to reflect on the events of your life and your reaction to them, do you find your reflections helpful and illuminating or do you become defensive and react by re-litigating the events and conversations? Often we just have an ongoing argument in our head – "he said, she said; I want or don't want; yada yada yada…"

One of the biggest reasons to begin this kind of investigation is to discover that these thoughts are running your life and they come from an unexamined source - your own, personal story. Can you interrupt the fixation on the relationship drama and the belief that achieving the good life always seems to be riding on what you do or don't do?

The invitation is again
to ask, "What does Love see"?

Why do any of this in-depth looking into your life? For me, it was emotional stress and the pain I felt when it seemed "things went wrong".

Many on this path of self-inquiry say pain pushes while truth pulls. I did not like the pain and wanted to be interested in Truth pulling me towards peace and happiness. So I was motivated from about my late 20s. It doesn't matter when one "wakes up" but I do think if you are seeking and open you will feel the pull.

If it's just, "let me get through this…job, upset, relationship trauma, financial difficulty, etc., you will use your willpower to muscle through the situation. Many people do that – seemingly indifferent to questions about the purpose of their existence and the purpose of life.

For example, my husband had a life-threatening situation every decade of his life. First, he almost died from a ruptured appendix. Later he was trapped in the MGM Grand Las Vegas hotel fire. He had to escape on his hands and knees following a fireman. He just barreled through never seeming to get in touch with his feelings or sharing how these things changed him. And there were other times he used sheer fortitude to push himself.

I can't be a judge of the way he lived his life because I don't know what he learned. He was a loving, kind man, a great father and a successful businessman. Could he have enjoyed more peace, or perhaps more harmony and not died at an early age? Maybe…

Pondering his life is just the way a wife might do after 42 years together. My personal life seemed to be more of a struggle and it would have been so easy to give up and just be content with the status quo. From a human standpoint, everything looked great.

But something deep inside has always been "calling" to me. I just felt something was beckoning me even when life seemed to fall apart – especially after his death.

Staying the course of that inner direction has blessed me continually in every way. It is a much lived experience of seeing deeper that causes me to want to share with others in my life.

> *Investigate the "I" on whose behalf the search for peace and happiness arises. That is, turn your attention upon yourself and investigate who you really are, and in this way bring yourself back to the experiential understanding that you always and already are the awareness that you seek. All the peace and happiness you long for resides there.* [2]

Now it's your turn! With an honesty that holds nothing back – tell yourself the truth about yourself. Who do you think you are and why are you living a particular life?

No matter how it looks, it is your life and it knows the way home. Some may say, "Hey – I'm great and everything is perfect." Ok, I'd say, but keep asking yourself for more. Not as a judge but as a loving friend or parent - someone who deeply cares for you.

---

[2] You are the Happiness You Seek by Rupert Spira

I'm 80 and only recently did I say to myself, "I **really** like you!" What that means is for me to decipher, but at that moment, I felt loved!

When we discover who we truly are in life, it's said we become a beneficial presence. We get a glimpse of what love sees. What blesses one blesses all.

"Look with God
into the mirror
and see Him reflected.
This is life and true vision"
- (Mary Baker Eddy)

Chapter III - *PAUSE PAGE*

What is self-inquiry?

Do I have any thoughts or ideas that keep me from being happy?

Romans 8:16 & 17

Chapter IV: Breakdown/Breakthrough

Moving Beyond Myself

When we face ourselves, we witness that not only do we seem to have a separate life of our own but we feel we are the creators and originators of life. Just notice how you have a situation in daily life that feels captivating enough for you to create a story around the experience.

You are the star (even if it is a dream) and you tell the story to a friend, parent, lover or anyone that will listen. It could be a happy story, a painful one or a drama. The emotion associated with the theme doesn't matter. What does matter is that you are separate, alone and ruminating about your hopes, fears, concerns and grievances.

If the scene does not shift and change you might see that you aren't interested in seeing truthfully. The need has been to keep the attention focused on "me and my story". But we are talking about waking up in life and seeing that you are so much more than your story.

For me, it meant letting go of my God story and my sense of being separate, alone and isolated. Even if I was happy and peaceful it never lasted because I was starting from the premise of being a separate person alone in my skin.

Someone asked me if the universe is loving. I had to answer yes even if it appeared flawed and cruel. If it's loving then what about the brutality; the rape and murder, the plagues, the destructive forces of weather, man's inhumanity to man? Many of us use this to fuel our doubt. The old question, "If there is a God and He is good, then why so much evil in the world?"

Forgetting for the moment that you have seen goodness and love, you turn away and become the doubter once again. But the doubt is a signal you need to turn your thoughts inward to a level of higher awareness.

Your personal story is all you know and what you know seems better than stepping into the unknown. After all, life is about survival, right? Busy making a living, feeding, clothing, sheltering yourself and maybe a family takes all of your waking hours. Maybe you steal some time to entertain yourself or exercise or take a vacation. But you know you have to get back on the treadmill. Even if you have some freedom and have a more creative, expansive existence you are still striving for happiness, peace and maintaining your bodily health. Never far from thought is the nagging perennial question, how to keep death at bay?

I've never doubted for long that life was good. I did feel I wasn't always able to see that good. My old joke to myself was to "keep looking – there is a pony under the mess somewhere." But the personal sense of being a mortal who had to suffer, struggle and somehow be redeemed was my belief even though I had faith that life was good.

After all the years of study, I still felt like a spiritual seeker who needed…- what? Very often, it takes a big blow for the ego to surrender such as a financial crisis, divorce, health crisis and even death.

Many people in society have shared how life imploded and they fell apart or wanted to kill themselves due to extreme upheavals. After these past few years of isolation because of the pandemic, we have witnessed many destructive behaviors in the world.

But these experiences in life are just a distraction from the truth. The breakdowns present an opportunity to challenge our thoughts and our suffering.

The breakdown is not the end of the story but the potential for a breakthrough and the beginning of a new story.

My own particular breakdown/breakthrough began to emerge when my husband's illness was pronounced as "incurable". The idea of something in your life coming to "visit" with a delivery of an irreconcilable event can be anything. It depends on who you think you are at the moment and what comes to reveal itself. In our case, it was impending death.

After many months of dealing with serious but unexplained symptoms, finally, at USC Norris, we were in front of a renowned physician. We were seated side-by-side but miles apart in our thoughts, I'm sure. The tests that were recommended were run on my husband's blood and they were all the same as the others, but the big difference now was that the blood had to be kept warm for this malady to be diagnosed.

Well… (*as we held our breaths*) … the doctor said, "I have good news and bad news." How cliché. "The good news is I know what it is, Waldenstrom Macroglobulinemia and I can help you, but the bad news is that it is incurable."

The impact of those last words delivered, after being told there is hope and help, was like being run over by a big Mack truck in a matter of seconds. Bam, you're dead, but you did see light just for a brief moment.

Hope was there! We were only 52 and thought we would have many years together enjoying life as a relatively young couple. He was retired and I had retired from nursing and the children were on their own. How could this sentence of "incurable" be ours? It was <u>ours</u>, not just his. We had been together since we were 19 years old. We had grown up together and I had no idea how to live alone.

Sometimes when you are in shock and feel terror you become strong like steel. I felt like that – rigid and cold so I would not fall apart.

Karl never really showed his feelings very well – he was a businessman and had been able to run a company successfully and not by being all warm and fuzzy. He had already been steel. I had been warm and soft and maybe even fuzzy, but not now.

I asked him as we struggled through the next twelve years in and out of the Cancer Center at St. Joseph's and Norris, "How can you be so joyful?" He instantly responded, "Jan, they saved my life!"

He had been a super patient, working diligently with the doctor to keep track of his blood counts and tests. He lived normally once they found a temporary treatment. He played tennis and golf and he managed his business affairs. Even his friends didn't know he was sick.

I, on the other hand, felt fear and terror because all I could see was him with a death sentence. How would I manage to live alone when he died? He had been a great husband but he felt he had to control and manage our lives. The financial part of our marriage was a mystery to me.

He said, "You take care of our family and the spiritual side and I'll do the business side." And so we did that – until now. How would I live without my partner of 30 years?

So you can understand that our limited viewpoints originated from our separate, isolated selves. He felt relief that they had saved his life. I was stuck with "something will take his life from me." Both of us were living in a sense of ego - separate from the good.

I had been studying spiritual ideas since my mid-30s when I saw clearly in a flash that I had lived as a victim and that my God was too small. But even all those years later after that first awakening, I still felt alone and separate from Love!

A new sense of awakening was coming but it only felt strange and bad – a foreboding. I talked with my spiritual counselors weekly. I prayed that I'd be lifted out of this impending doom and that he would miraculously be healed. It was an existence filled with fear and sadness for me and finally depression.

This entire health crisis story is only one of the many ways life can seem to throw you a curve ball of experience that you don't know how to handle. As I said before, it could be a relationship crisis or financial problems and many other areas that come to assist in our seeing Life as it truly is.

For now, I'll speak of health – mental health and breakdowns manifesting as sleeplessness, anxiety and depression. Depression was my unconscious way to cope with uncertainty. Depression, sadness, fear and worry were all words my birth family used often. That emotional thread seemed to be the words used to describe and handle stressful situations. I had learned that way to cope with life.

The first time I remember being depressed, I was 16 years old and my father's work had transferred him and our family of six from a small town (population 800) to a small thriving city near a naval air station and oil refineries. We all felt lost and adrift.

I was a young impressionable girl who at an earlier age had decided God was the way and Jesus was my savior. So even though I felt lost I did have church and school friends.

I remember being on my knees pleading with God to help me get to school and to move past the feelings that robbed me of joy. At this point, I just needed to cope with life.

The next time depression showed up was after the birth of each of my three children. It was mild but I couldn't leave my home for weeks. Sleep deprivation from the baby's schedule contributed to those feelings of depression as well. The blessing of being freed from that depression always saved me. I didn't know why but it always lifted. I recovered my sense of well-being and gave the situation little thought that it might reoccur. I just put it out of my mind.

Until more recent years, post-partum depression wasn't seen as a serious condition. My mother had serious depression after my birth and was given shock therapy. She never got over the stigma of that experience. Still, knowing this, I had not become alarmed or concerned for my mental health. The next three decades of my life revealed the depth that the depressed state could take me.

In my 40s, I had a period of anxiety, sleeplessness and depression that was severe enough to require hospitalization. I felt helpless and unable to function. So my doctor felt a time in the hospital psychiatric ward with meds and observation would help. After a month's stay, I was home and feeling well again.

Once more I had a sense of relief since I had been in therapy for years just to gain clarity and balance in my emotional health. But I began to suspect these depressions were heralding an invitation into a spiritual awakening I had not known.

It wasn't just a medical condition to be dealt with now. I had heard of the "dark night of the Soul" and when I had another plunge into anxiety and sleeplessness so severe that I could not control the energy in my body, I became very fearful. Once more, I was hospitalized for several weeks.

What if I was going insane? My mother had similar fears and this felt like a thought planted and feared only to come true. I have heard several times, "Be careful of what you fear, cherish or hate as it may come true in your experience".

Returning home after the second hospital stay and feeling some relief, life seemed normal once more. It was beautiful to see that despite my breakdowns; my children were doing well - completing college and getting married. They seemed unaffected and were establishing lives of their own.

My husband had successfully closed his business of twenty years and retired. All seemed well until he was suddenly diagnosed with an incurable rare blood disease. Even though he was able to live a relatively normal life for 12 years while in treatment, for me, his medical challenges and the death sentence brought a sense of foreboding that never went away.

Eventually, Karl's treatment lost its ability to control the cancer. The doctor recommended surgery which while successful, resulted in complications that kept him in the ICU for the month before his death.

The time after a loved one's death is full of tasks to be handled which I did with the help of my children. In time, the crisis passed and while each one of us suffered in different ways, everyone got back to their everyday lives and I was left alone for the first time in my life.

I can't explain it but about three years after his death I began to feel the old familiar anxiety and sleeplessness that heralded the other depressions. It was frightening and I knew I couldn't go into a hospital setting again. But I needed help!

A friend suggested a residential facility that provided support and care for those who are struggling with anxiety and depression. Only later did I learn that the facility probably leaned towards helping people with addictions, primarily alcohol.

My son and I were frightened and I was desperate and we did not thoroughly investigate this facility where I paid cash to stay without fully understanding the contract or without checking with my insurance.

I had my medication for anxiety but my anxiety escalated right after I checked in. Within a few hours, the staff of the residential facility was concerned that they were not qualified to deal with my condition. As a result the psychiatrist on staff, who also ran a local hospital, decided I should go there immediately.

Upon admission, I was asked if I was committing myself. Even in my state of confusion, I can remember that question. I said “yes”, but had no idea what that meant – that treatment for addiction requires the consent of the patient.

I was not an alcoholic and did not take drugs. I was a terrified woman who was fearful of another severe breakdown and depression. I feel they misdiagnosed me and treated me with drugs and a bed and safety from potential suicide. Suicidal thoughts had come to me before but I don’t think I would have had the courage to act on them. I was just so tired of this repeated pattern and it not going away. I was desperate.

The memories of not being respected and treated like an object during my hospital stay remain with me. It was not about the patients having the best care. I can still see the shadow of who I thought I was fading as I didn’t want to bathe and only dressed in wrinkled old clothes. Meals were communal and many patients were unable to feed themselves competently, dribbling food onto their laps. I felt disgusted with them and with myself and I felt abandoned by family and friends.

It wasn't *One Flew Over the Cuckoo's Nest* but it was a locked-down facility. I felt this time I was going "mad" and one night in sleeplessness I could imagine hell, the devil and that I was there – in hell.

Towards the end of my stay, I was moved to another room and while waiting for the aides to change my bed I began to talk to a cleaning staff individual. The other patient admitted to this new room was clearly in DTs (delirium tremors) and I made mention of this to the person cleaning. She said, "Oh, we have people like that all the time in alcohol withdrawal." **OMG** – they had seen me as that kind of patient because of the facility I had been transferred from! It was a humiliating and degrading experience.

Finally, after several weeks and for a reason I don't know, I was discharged. A doctor came in, looked me over quickly, discharged me and said simply, "good luck." No advice or directives, no referrals. Just, "good luck". I can still hear that message in my mind and the feeling of, what does that mean? **Doomed**. You are on your own and good riddance!

My daughter took me to my apartment and we both realized that I could not be left living alone. My niece is a nurse and she was asked to stay with me which meant a trip from Michigan for a stay of two weeks.

Graciously she came and tried her best to calm me down but to no avail. For two weeks, she cared for me, cooking, loving, trying to get me to eat, bathe and walk or move in any kind of way.

I did return to a psychiatrist I had seen many years before. While he wasn't necessarily helpful, he could prescribe medications and he did, trying new drugs and even really listening for a while. I went back the following weeks, the same song, 100th verse and it was getting very old and disheartening.

One day after my appointment with him we went to the pharmacy to get another drug. It had a warning about becoming addicted and someone had said I was addicted - paranoid again. I argued with my niece from 3:00 p.m. until 3:00 a.m. about taking the medication. She was the nurse and I must take the pill, dammit! I was a paranoid patient and refused. If this was happening in a play or novel, we would call it a 'tragicomedy'. Finally, after two weeks, she chose to go home, defeated, and exhausted.

Meanwhile, my daughter contacted the residential facility and insisted they honor their contract with me by providing services in my home. Someone to cook meals and I remember they sent counselors and a spiritual guide of sorts. It seemed most of them must have been recovered alcoholics by how they spoke to me even encouraging me to admit I had an alcohol problem. I had gone to that center and not had any idea what they were set up to provide.

One counselor came and, after being with me over the month, said, "I can't see how your home and environment reflect such quality if you are so ill. I kept having the thought, "you people are talking *AT* me and have no idea that I know all the lingo. **I can see the truth but I'm somehow locked from living the awareness of it. Where was I?**

This was my soul asking I think. Where are you? One of the thoughts running through my mind was, "**I can't live and I can't die.**" I was doomed for certain and saw no way out of the abyss.

The dark night of the soul is a term that speaks well of my journey. It is a soul journey and it is very dark. You feel you've been cast aside, thrown to the wolves, so to speak, to survive on your own. I couldn't think clearly or reference any ideas from all my spiritual seeking and studying. I was in the desert with no hope.

Nothing made sense anymore and I felt my mother's (and now my) greatest fear had come true. I had lost my mind, I was insane! Any support I had felt before seemed to disappear as family and friends stopped calling or stopped checking in on me. One faithful friend (even now) continued to call and express love. I can still hear the voices of what I thought everyone felt – "Why can't you be like you were? **Where did you go?"**

Given my dire circumstances, I could not seem to function on my own so a caregiver was hired. I had expressed suicidal tendencies before but now I was not present enough to even consider that terrible idea. I would sit for hours, not eat or bathe and needed someone near me for basic comfort and care.

My other greatest fear was cancer. To add insult to injury I had a medical issue needing a hysterectomy when the doctor said it was stage 1 uterine cancer. Thankfully I only needed surgery and 5 years of follow-up.

But my husband's recent death was the biggest fear. How would I function without my life partner? My life had imploded and I no longer existed. Indeed **where was "I"?**

The idea of an
existential surrender
felt like it could be the key.

These questioning thoughts were different from suffering thoughts. Throughout the mental breakdowns over the years I've held in my awareness that this journey was spiritual and not mental.

When people ask how I was lifted out of this dark night, I say I don't know except it had to be from a depth of surrender that wasn't from the ego. Can there be a divine surrender based on a foundation of truth being loved and valued? I say YES! I find great hope in that and my miraculous recovery has become my assurance and promise.

To return to the downfall one last time (this has been difficult to revisit) – I was living with a caregiver for at least a year, seeing a psychiatrist and taking medication but never really improving. Finally, at my daughter's insistence, I sought out a new counselor - a graduate of The University of Santa Monica program in spiritual psychology run by the Hulnicks.[3]

With resignation and a defeated heart I went and confessed to my new therapist – "I've told my story so many times that it bores even me in this state of mind." After a couple of months, she said I think you are overmedicated. I heartily agreed but did not have the will on my own to stop taking the prescribed pills.

After a brief consultation, we decided it would be ok for her to make an appointment with a doctor in Laguna Niguel that was doing research on the brain and how drugs affected its function. Together we began a new tactic of getting me off psyche drugs.

Within a few months, gradually reducing the medications, I said I don't need anything to alter my brain anymore. That was it! No meds, no counselors! I was free in every way. There was no depression, no sadness, no fear. The fear I had lived with all my life had been lifted! It was gone. **All I felt was joy and freedom**.

No person had done anything. It just felt like a spell had lifted and I was a new being. No longer a fearful, struggling person, I was free! "*And the truth will set you free*" (John 8:31-33)

---

[3] https://www.universityofsantamonica.edu/about/

When I go over the story in my mind, it always feels like a miracle. That's the way it comes – a lifting from the dark night into daylight. I could finally SEE and what I saw was love, beauty and harmony - all of life's possibilities. This was GRACE!

I had been living in a great apartment where I could walk to Balboa Island and even see the ocean. But, it was time to leave now. I knew I wanted a home of my own and by February I had purchased a townhome. That also felt like a gift! It was perfect!

My new awakened sense
was engaged but now
***Life was living me*.**

There had been no way out, nothing could be done humanly to lift me out and up into Life. No personal prayers. It wasn't a person knowing there was only God.

It is a mystery in a way as I thought I was doomed. The family history of melancholy and depression (even a suicide) said it was impossible to be free. My new understanding did not come from pleading with a god somewhere out there. It was a gift for which I will be eternally grateful.

During this dark journey, I felt invisible to everyone – especially to myself. But **LOVE** saw me! I felt healed! It felt like I was being lifted up and out of a depressed state and into the awareness of joy with a freedom from fear that I had never known. I was vibrantly alive. I may never comprehend the full journey but it put me on a trajectory of openness and trust that never seems to change. I will listen and learn always knowing there is only the One Life living itself as an idea called Spiritual Man.

If you have read this far and gotten through one human's drama, you may be asking, what does the question, "What does love see" reveal? This turning point now provides a new way to see Life, giving you a new perspective and great hope.

Suffering humanity is the norm but what if we don't have to live this way – striving, seeking, and suffering? Life living itself can be joyful, harmonious, efficient, effective and effortless.

If you've been brave enough to slow down and question your values, you may be willing to stop and listen. Ask yourself – am I happy? **What does Love see?**

Ask yourself –
Am I happy?
What does Love see?

Chapter IV - *PAUSE PAGE*

Do I know what happiness is?

Can I live in peace and harmony?

Is being joyful a possibility?

Now give some thought about the moment in your life when you were no longer in charge or in control of your personal life.

Did you have a breakthrough?

(*Luke 1:37*)

"Coming Home"

Chapter V: Coming Home to Yourself

The Journey Already Happening

The first half of this book was an invitation to look at who you believed yourself to be and how you held yourself in the world. Unfolding my storyline and revealing thoughts I believed, demonstrated to me the life that felt too small for me. My journey of self-inquiry led to the unveiling of a new and real possibility of Life living me. I believe this journey is available to all beings.

It is not about a religious journey although that was my path, Christianity in particular. I have seen how all the ideas I believed were stepping stones, building blocks that helped to open my eyes.

Nothing you've lived
is wasted.

I'm not a theologian or a student of religion or philosophy. My urging, 45 years ago, was an inner direction to observe my own life and learn to inquire at that depth. It would guide me if I would only be still, fearless and open to the truth of what unfolded. This self-inquiry is available to you also.

I realized my inquiry would require some guidance and initially it was grace that led me to Metapsychiatry by Dr. Thomas Hora. The counselors that were trained by him shared this work. They were professional and very spiritual, doing their own inner work and they helped me to begin.

On this pilgrimage, I encountered other teachings such as those of Joel Goldsmith and his Infinite Way, A Course in Miracles, Gerald Jampolsky, MD, Mary Baker Eddy, John Hargreaves, and Margaret Laird.

I had been trained as a registered nurse and began to see that our body, while a miracle in itself, was a starting point for seeing beyond the physical. So I took many classes from physicians, spiritual healers and like-minded souls - all searching.

Gathering insight when my mother was approaching her death, I found myself questioning how Western medicine had counseled and treated her as a patient. Had they helped? Could there be something more? Death began to be a mystery rather than a fearful threat.

I was being led into more depth but I didn't realize it at the time. My inner questions arose and then I would see an unfolding idea that seemed to call me. It wasn't like trying things as a fad.

The basis of my yearning felt grounded in love and truth. Honesty and integrity were my family's "badge of honor" as my father was big on following the rules and telling the truth. So I had a childhood foundation of the importance of good values and then wonderful spiritual guides on my search for understanding. Your reflections will reveal your foundations.

My study was a letting go gradually of all my old beliefs in hopes of seeing with new eyes. I heard stories of the ego dropping completely and almost overnight for some of our current teachers revealing higher ideas and understanding.

I was very interested in truth, but I am an ordinary woman with an ordinary tale. I had no extraordinary revelations. If you feel the same, I hope to encourage you. We can all do this! By seeking to learn a new perspective, we will find the truth about ourselves – we are spiritual beings even if we are having an ordinary life. And, we are already home.

Jesus' story was an example and always called me but now it seemed to say, don't just follow me, you need to do as I did and know who you are. The kingdom of God (i.e. Life) is within and it is the pearl of great price. (Luke 17:20-21)

My understanding is that the way is open to be discovered. Life is inviting us to come home. It is available to all and we are all welcome. We only need to accept the invitation and realize our true identity.

For me, it was about being honest with myself and saying "Yes!" I knew I needed help as I began to seek understanding but I wasn't sure what that help was.

All my life I had tried to be truthful but this honesty was taking me to a new place. If as a human being I've spent my life creating a persona so my ego could feel confident, what would "honesty" feel like without the mask, the persona?

There is an inner listening to a still small voice that is trying to speak loudly enough to be heard. An example could be seen as a mature adult working to cultivate close relationships in a marriage, with a family and a job.

How many times a day do you have an interaction where you feel something is off in your thinking but you "sweep the thought under the rug" so to speak? You are in a hurry and it wasn't a major issue just a slight gnawing in the gut that said that's not ok. Now compound that with days and weeks and even months passing where you eventually stop noticing.

Honesty is the key
and forgiveness is the gift in
this process.

We just need to stop and see with new eyes. Honesty with yourself would have prompted inquiry and maybe a new action and possibly peace. Is it worth the time to stop and notice? Signs are everywhere in daily life.

This kind of honesty led me to the importance of humility that can initiate healing within and without. But if you find a good counselor or spiritual guide to assist you and you only tell them what you think sounds good, then you have short-changed yourself. They get paid but you have lost the moment.

This brings up integrity. What does integrity have to do with me? Isn't that what politicians and lawyers and doctors need to possess to interact with constituents or clients?

Integrity is defined as *the quality of being honest and having strong moral principles.* We see where lack of integrity in our world has led to distrust and even destruction of lives, property and world peace.

The second definition of integrity is *the state of being whole and undivided.* If I have integrity in life then that radiates out into the world as peace, assurance, gratitude and love even in a small way. But it starts with me. Is it possible to live this life?

When I come to SEE what Love sees regarding honesty and integrity it points to the One. There is the One Life living itself here and now.

It is my life now and it feels like coming home to myself. Jesus made this very point when he said, *"I am in the Father and the Father is in me"* (John 14:11). Once again, he was expressing his identity.

My life has taken on reality - no longer feared or pushed away and hidden out of guilt and shame. It is the greatest gift to start in thought as a spiritual being, as Principle – another name for God. When you start with the truth, you always end up with the truth. But an error in the premise (of your equation) leads only to an error in the conclusion. Repeating this phrase to myself has helped me stay awake to who is speaking (error or truth) and stay alert to the habitual thought patterns of the past trying to reclaim footing in my life. It becomes a practice!

There are so many resources on the planet that are easily available to assist with mindfulness. If we are seriously searching, we can see our Oneness unveiling in our world now. The internet has made this possible more than ever before. These available resources are the seeds that hold the promise of growth and maturity. In a famous parable, Jesus explained that not all available wisdom (seeds) finds fertile minds (good soil) but when it does, a bounteous crop of goodness happens. (Matthew 13:20-22)

In our particular time, we are blessed with men and women experiencing consciousness expanding and sharing what they have come to understand regarding the world at large. In coming home to see what Love sees we are going beyond narrow-minded beliefs and limited concepts. We are awake and welcoming an understanding of conscious awareness that is larger than the life we have known.

A contemporary teacher, Eckhart Tolle, defined the reality of Truth and Love he experienced in his book, The New Earth. He had an awakening experience where his ego dropped and he saw things completely anew.

Byron Katie also had a life-transforming awakening and was given "The Work" to share. She invites us to question our thoughts in a logical way that can move us out of our self-created torment.

Deepak Chopra is a leading physician who invites us to question our beliefs about the body, health and even death. Rupert Spira teaches profoundly the essence of non-duality. So many current teachers of truth have offered tools to help see through past suffering to a life expressed in happiness and peace.

This awareness of happiness and peace is a natural state when we discover we are already home as conscious awareness. It has felt like a journey to me, but now I see I AM home.

It has felt
like a
journey
to me
but now
I see
***I AM** home.*

Chapter V - *PAUSE PAGE*

Integrity is a quality of being. It means holding on, at all times to your highest sense of truth and your vision, whatever the cost may be. It consists in resonating with the most intimate fiber of your being which enjoins us not to withdraw one inch, whatever the prestige or authority of the person or institution opposing us. And this, not out of obstinacy, but because of the quiet courage in an inner voice which says: "This above all: to thine own self be true…" [4]

What does "to thine own self be true" mean to me?

[4] Unbroken Wholeness by Pierre Pradervand

Chapter VI: The Practice

Daily Contemplation

The Practice seems to begin when you first realize that life is more than you thought. You begin to have renewed curiosity about yourself – who you are and what your real purpose might be. It pulls you! This new awareness seems to invite you in but it is very subtle. For most people, this seems to evolve over years of interest in truth.

There are periods of ardent desire to know and understand coupled with dry spells of complete distraction.

When we were young we were in schools of one sort or another. Then later our culture and environment seemed to promote finding a partner and working hard to survive. We married or not but we often paired off and isolated as a family. How busy we became.

For some of us, a gnawing unease within grew and we began to search for more insights. This seemed to become a practice of sorts. But in what direction were we journeying? And who am "I" that is on the journey?

Regardless of the era we live in, we have distractions that we need to overcome to have the chance to see the truth. In mid-life and moving into your 60s, there is often a mid-life crisis. Men may want a new, young partner or a different job - anything to rekindle that feeling of adventure and something to conquer.

From my own life experience, I have noticed that women of my era were still looking for independence and autonomy. This was especially true if they were in a long-term marriage. Now it seems women have decided they need no one and are completely independent.

Young men seem to struggle to find themselves as our society no longer promotes a common ritual for initiation into manhood and some have no strong male figure to emulate. Men often seem lost in our culture as their role of "protector" and "provider" has diminished.

What if all these "re-positionings" were a disguise and a distraction to keep you from your soul's journey? You may still be doing the same things, as habits die hard, but the understanding you search for can possibly bring new meaning to your life.

"The heart is restless… until it rests in Thee, Oh Lord" (St Augustine Confessions). Straddling the fence spiritually can reveal discord, disharmony and chaos in your personal life. Some are so sensitive they have to shut down and check out entirely. I often wonder if this isn't revealed as homelessness and poverty. "Life is just too hard and the surrender is on a human level, so 'I just quit!'"

Others struggle and since now it is acceptable to break down emotionally and go to therapists and counselors, we have another diversion. Many have physical ailments and become convinced it is just a disease of the body forgetting and blocking out the mind's turmoil and confusion. Years are dedicated to keeping the body alive.

If you have gone through marriage and raising a family, completing years of endless (often unrewarding) work and been blessed to have arrived at an older age, you have a new job! Your mind and time become occupied with sorting out and trying to contemplate what aging in a healthy way means.

In this stage, you seem on the "other side" of some invisible time frame and approaching death. Our distractions evolve but they are always an opportunity to look beyond and see the truth of life.

What does any of this have to do with the "Practice"? In my way of thinking, a spiritual practice has carried me through all those adventures to having a disciplined focus! Taking time each day for mindful contemplation makes a difference. For me it is loving the idea of a higher conscious awareness that I have always called God. Now it is aware presence of One Life living me. It has carried me through life no matter what experiences came and went.

When challenged to put this into words, really it becomes impossible to say, "I know because…" It is a felt sense and an inner knowledge I would call understanding.

At the beginning of the journey, I called it intuition, then faith and hope but now I rest in understanding that I am a spiritual being.

We, in this world, are spiritual beings having a human experience until we wake to see what LOVE Sees.
Love Sees Itself.

I live a new vibrancy even at 80 years old and I feel the possibility of Life living what I have called me. I feel more joy and happiness as I contemplate Oneness.

The false beliefs about mankind are being revealed in violent ways in our lives now. Instead of the truth, we see wars, conflicts, struggles of every sort that are pointing towards the opposite of Oneness. More distractions! What we long for is peace, harmony and the true brotherhood of mankind. Often people do not see that and get caught up in distractions that blind them but there is more if we can gain a new perspective.

A practice, a focus with vision of a loving Principle calls us home to rest in safety and security. Create your own practice and work with a guide or counselor that is clearly on the same path if you need it. I always needed and appreciated the direction of guidance.

This is a road less traveled, and not easy, but it is so worth the journey. The evidence that we are home is the felt sense of life lived with the qualities of love, joy, peace, long-suffering, gentleness, goodness and faith. These are the fruits of the spirit "against which there is no law". (Galatians 5:22)

Noticing these qualities as a guide gives a sense "that all is well and all manner of things shall be well" (St Theresa of Avila). Practice asks, "What does Love see in this moment?" not "what does a false personality see?"

Look within for a quality life. But how to get to that point? I had to become aware initially that I needed to learn to listen to my body by different physical practices.

The first classes I took were, Touch for Health, Edu-Kinesthetic, Focusing and then I completed a series of Rolfing sessions. Then I learned Tai Chi Chih. Reiki revealed another depth of healing bodywork. Also, I have practiced Iyengar Yoga. All of these disciplines were pointing me towards wholeness and developing my own daily practice of being still enough to listen within without fear.

I had already realized how my thoughts were trying to run my life. Now, being conscious of my body/mind connections a new depth of wholeness was revealed.

Each person seems to find their own way to become more awake and aware. Some people go out in nature and walk consciously. The particular discipline needed will reveal itself as you begin to enjoy harmony and order and the truth of being more than a sense of a separate suffering self.

Don't worry about what to do and how to do it. Just become interested, curious and open. The truth is that Love and Grace do all the work to bring you to your inherent happiness.

Be kind to yourself and give the gift of time spent in quiet reflection. Find the truth that sustains you and devote periods of contemplation until it becomes a way of life – a practice.

Love is the way!

Chapter VI - *Pause Page*

An Example of a Practice

Mindful contemplation – What Love Sees
Breathe in, breathe out

When I spend time in my contemplative practice it brings:

- increased awareness of my surroundings,
- possibility of being more present with people,
- helps me shut out distractions,
- settles my unquiet mind,
- a noticing of soft sounds, textures &colors.

This results in a brighter, more vibrant and keener sense of aliveness.

My awareness of God's goodness and love and the Oneness of Being increases my patience, kindness, generosity and forgiveness in my world.

What is your practice for daily contemplation?

Do you have a body discipline of quiet movement like Tai Chi or Yoga?

Do you get distracted by new ideas and try to follow too many?

Chapter VII: Soul Work

The End that is really the Beginning

*You have come to the end of one story only to begin your own by asking yourself, "**What is Love**?"*

How do I know what Love **sees** if I don't know what it is? We can start with an investigation into the definition of love that we have come to believe in our culture. But a true investigation holds the promise of a deeper understanding – a felt understanding.

At this point you have words and concepts that only refer to a belief about love. We have grown up with and most often express the love within family, between friends, romantic love and married love. It still misses the mark.

In questioning your beliefs about love, you have truly opened a new door of discovery. When you ask what love sees you become open to the idea that Love is a synonym for God.

The invitation is to let a new awareness expand to fill the field of thought. Your thinking mind will probably say, "What a lofty thought!" But why not risk this moment of revelation with the possibility of having a new vision – the awareness of seeing the One Life as the only Life?

When a mentor asked me to consider what love sees and not what separate sense sees, I was at another beginning place. Many years ago I was given a brilliant definition of love by Dr. Thomas Hora in his book Beyond the Dream. "Love is non-conditional, non-personal benevolence". I now desire to live those words as a place where love expresses itself in life by being as present as possible – moment by moment.

Recently, I was blessed to have a dialogue with a friend where these ideas could be explored. At precisely 5:28pm a tall, handsome younger man arrived at my door. He married a friend of mine 25 years ago and now we are having an evening to explore this idea of Love through friendly conversation.

We three had dinner together several weeks earlier and I mentioned I was writing a book entitled, What Does Love See? I shared that this was a profound question presented to me to ponder at a time when I was looking at some family dynamics that were causing me difficulties. As my friend walks in we greet one another and he asks me with a slight challenge in his tone of voice, "**Well, what does Love See**?"

I realize from his question that this will be a wonderful evening as we dialogue about spiritual ideas. He really wants an answer and we hang on to that question all evening as we explore the idea of consciousness and walking through what he calls an invisible door into an unknown realm.

What kind of faith do you have to possess to take a step and ask, "Who am I if I'm not my story?"

What happens in life that wakes you up to some larger idea beyond your beliefs? "What am I, where am I and what is my purpose in life?" These are life-changing questions that stop you right where you are – both mentally and physically.

I shared with my friend that for me, I found myself in a suffering sense in my 30s and I knew I wanted harmony and peace. Having begun this journey as a religious individual, I thought immediately of God. If I could just figure out who God was and who I was maybe I could have some rest and feel safe and secure. A large task! Impossible? No! Little did I understand back then what a challenging but worthwhile spiritual journey I would be taking.

"I am not suffering," he says and he does seem happy and sure of himself. He shares that he realizes that life is more than survival. "I know that most of us work too hard and don't slow down enough to really be present to a vibrant life." "How do you step through that invisible door to a spiritual awakening? Is anyone there? Will it reveal hidden demons to be conquered?" What a thoughtful man, with deep questions.

What does Love see?
It seems to me that this is not a question so much answered as one that you hold close as you go about daily life and allow it to live you.

The world seems to offer many challenges every moment. Everywhere there is crisis now. Democracy is challenged by fighting factions fueled by lies not by truth. The pandemic is causing people to live in fear and isolation and confusion. The climate appears to be rebelling with fires and floods, hurricanes, earthquakes and tornadoes just to mention the grand scheme of current disasters. The internet and social media connects us in a blink of an eye but we are increasingly at a loss for true understanding. There seems to be threats everywhere. There are wars and rumors of wars.

It is hard to feel safe and know our safety is real and enduring. So humans frantically keep themselves busy with distractions (family relationships, work, play, and health crises) anything to focus on so you don't have to confront the existential fear.

Even in this conversation between two friends, we chose to stop and face any fear and asked a bigger question about Love. What is it? And if I ask what love sees do I get new answers that will open my eyes to have a new perspective and **really SEE**?

I feel this question propels me into another way of looking past the impulse to always confirm my own separate self. That self is too small for the beautiful soul sincerely seeking a new answer, a new way.

By just asking how your own personal inner commentary can lead you down a self-confirming path, you can start to see an alternative and begin to allow Life to live you. With integrity and honesty you open the door that only you had shut tight.

Maybe it seems smug on my part but I have walked this road less traveled and I have come to see beyond my story and personhood enough to know this journey is valuable beyond measure. I say this to my friend as the evening ends wanting to offer assurance and encouragement.

Each of us has our own thoughts and definitions of Love and Soul which we express as opinions and beliefs. But when confronted with a situation in your life, go beyond that and truly ask, “What does Love see here?”

If your only perspective is from you as an individual person, separate from Love and Good, and asking what you see, your answer will only reflect who you believe you are. What if there is more?

This feels like a new beginning and it is! The awakening to what Love sees is the beginning of the end of our separate ego image. You are invited once again to take a step, open the door and stay open in your heart, living in the question of what Love sees.

It seems to me that
Love Sees Itself
and Love never fails!

Chapter VII - *PAUSE PAGE*

"What we call the beginning
Is often the end
And to make an end is
To make a beginning" (T.S. Elliot)

How would you define Love?

Are you beginning to see that you are Love, seeing itself?

How can one become a loving beneficial presence and "place of service"?

I am the Alpha and the Omega – the beginning and the end (Revelations 22:13). This represents the completeness of Being.

(1 John 4:16)

Recommended Books

*Love is Letting Go of Fear & Teach Only Love: Twelve Principles of Attitudinal Healing by Gerald G. Jampolsky

...... total giving and total acceptance are crucial to the healing process and that attitudinal healing can lead to harmony, joy and life without fear

The Course in Miracles by Foundation for Inner Peace

...... a channeled view of Life

*The Road Less Traveled: A New Psychology of Love, Traditional Values and Spiritual Growth by Scott Peck

...... celebration of self-actualization, love and spiritual growth

The New Earth & The Power of Now by Eckhart Tolle

...... bringing spirituality to mainstream thought - awakening to your life's purpose

****Helpful for Beginners***

Beyond the Dream by Dr. Thomas Hora
...... "All problems are psychological, but all solutions are spiritual."

The Soul's Code: In Search of Character and Calling by James Hillman
...... a reasoned and powerful road map to understanding our true nature and discovering an eye-opening array of choices

The Bible – King James and New International versions

The Infinite Way and other books by Joel Goldsmith
...... "the kingdom of God is within you." (Luke 17:20-21)

Addresses and Other Writings on Christian Science by Doris Henty
...... spiritual healing

Ageless Body, Timeless Mind by Deepak Chopra
......There is nothing inevitable about aging
- information that can help us live long, healthy lives

Science and Health with Key to the Scriptures by Mary Baker Eddy

…… a new perspective on body/mind and health

"God is All-in all."

"God is good."

"God is Mind, and God is infinite; hence all is Mind."

As I See It by John Hargreaves

…… challenges the reader to raise the bar on their own sense of what consciousness is

Loving What Is: Four Questions That Can Change Your Life by Byron Katie

…… "The Work" – a practical tool for transformation

A Thousand Names for Joy: Living in Harmony with the Way Things Are by Byron Katie

…… a new vision and practical insight into discovering freedom

Loyalty to Your Soul: The Heart of Spiritual Psychology by H. Ronald Hulnick & Mary R. Hulnick

…… a workbook for discovery

Soul Kissed by Ann Linthorst
...... practical living

Radical Forgiveness by Colin Tipping
...... A five-stage process for true forgiveness, giving up blame

The Gentle Art of Blessing by Pierre Pradervand
...... living as a blessing of self and others

The Most Important Thing : Discovering Truth at the Heart of Life by Adyashanti
...... shows you how to look past your personal narratives, delve inward, and connect with the truths that fundamentally animate all of us

Presence Volumes I & II by Rupert Spira
...... consciousness is ALL, non-duality

The Poetry of David Whyte & the Poetry of Mary Oliver
...... seeing through the eyes of contemporary poets

ABOUT THE AUTHOR

Jan Kovac, RN, Health Facilitator, wife, mother, grandmother and great grandmother

As an Intensive Care nurse, Jan provided care for severely ill patients. Witnessing the deep needs of the patients and their families created a desire within her to discover what actual healing meant. By the time her mother died at an early age, Jan was convinced that the inner knowing about our own bodies was more important than the outer physical illness that was always the focus of western medicine.

So, Jan's path became focused on studying spiritual healing and alternative modalities. She became a Health Facilitator which involved really listening to clients.

In What Does Love See? Jan shares intimate details of her life, including her physical and emotional reactions to her early loves and losses, her husband's death from cancer and her bouts with what doctors diagnosed as depression and mental breakdown. She offers her own life journey and healing as an invitation to Life asking, "What Does Love See?" not, "What does the ego see?"

Although Jan went through a great deal of earnest study and honest searching, she still refers to herself as just an ordinary woman.

Acknowledging how her life journey is nothing less than a miraculous blessing, Jan wants to share this book with you – her reader – in very much the same way as she would enjoy a loving conversation over tea or coffee while sitting on her sofa. Imagine that as you read, and you'll come to know Jan and maybe something more of yourself!

"And the light shines
in darkness;
and the darkness
comprehended it not."
John 1:5

Printed in Great Britain
by Amazon